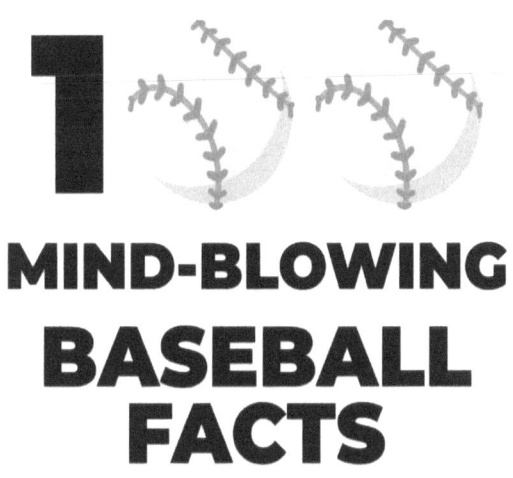

MIND-BLOWING
BASEBALL FACTS

100 Wild Stories from Baseball's Most Unpredictable Moments

FELIX GRAYSON

Copyright © 2025 by MindSpark Publishing

All rights reserved. No part of this book may be reproduced, stored in a retrieval system, or transmitted in any form or by any means—electronic, mechanical, photocopying, recording, or otherwise—without the prior written permission of the publisher, except in the case of brief quotations embodied in critical articles or reviews.

This book is intended to provide general information on the topics discussed and is not intended as a substitute for professional advice. Every effort has been made to ensure accuracy, but the author and publisher assume no responsibility for errors, omissions, or contrary interpretation of the subject matter.

Published by MindSpark Publishing.
Cover design by MindSpark Publishing.

CONTENTS

Before We Dive In… 8
Introduction 10
The Game That Refused to End 13
Babe Ruth's Home Run Buyback Program 15
The Day the Yankees Refused to Strike Out 17
The Case of the Missing Teeth 19
The Arm of a Machine: Nolan Ryan's 235-Pitch Marathon 21
The Strike Zone the Size of a Postcard 23
The Pitch That Killed 25
The Day a Woman Struck Out Babe Ruth 27
The Grand Slam That Never Landed 29
The Home Run That Left the Stadium… and the City 31
The Beer That Won a Batting Title 33
The Pitcher Who Threw a No-Hitter… on LSD 35
The Time a Game Was Delayed… by Swarming Bees! 37
The Batboy Who Got Ejected 39
The Mascot That Got Tackled by a Player 41
The World Series That Ended in an Earthquake 43
The Game That Was Played in Complete Silence 45
The Day a Pitcher Threw a No-Hitter… and Lost 47
The Time a Game Was Delayed… by an Umpire's Underwear 49
The Player Who Stole First Base… on Purpose 51
The Fan Who Caught Two Home Runs… in the Same Inning! 53

The Time a Pitcher Was Traded… for a Handful of Bats 55

The Time a Pitcher Threw a Perfect Game… While Drunk 57

The Player Who Hit a Home Run… and Missed Home Plate 59

The Game That Lasted Two Days… But Only One Inning 61

The Time a Pitcher Was Struck by Lightning… and Kept Playing .. 63

The World Series MVP Who Didn't Play a Single Game 65

The Time a Player Stole First Base… from Second! 67

The Home Run That Bounced Off a Player's Head 69

The Game That Ended With a Walk-Off… Grand Slam Single 71

The Player Who Hit Two Grand Slams… in the Same Inning 73

The Time a Manager Sent a Midget to Bat 75

The World Series That Ended With a Pickoff 77

The Day a Player Was Ejected for Not Smiling 79

The Player Who Took the Longest Walk 81

The Player Who Hit a Home Run Off a Broken Bat 83

The Player Who Ran the Bases in the Wrong Order 85

The Game Played With Only One Foul Ball 87

The Pitch That Defied Physics 89

The Player Who Hit a Home Run… and Got Hit by a Pitch! 91

The Time a Player Hit a Home Run Off the Stadium Scoreboard ... 93

The No-Hitter That Was Almost Perfect—But Not Quite 95

The Shortest Game Ever Played 97

The First-Ever Triple Play to End a World Series 99

The Game That Ended in a Tie… After 25 Innings! 101

The Baseball That Went Into Orbit (Almost) 103

The Player Who Played With a Broken Neck 105

The 100-Year-Old Baseball 107

The Game Played Without a Single Hit! 109

The Time a Bat Boy Hit a Home Run! 111

The Ball That Was Hit By Lightning 113

The Player Who Played the Most Games Without a Home Run 115

The Game Played Without a Single Pitcher 117

The Time a Player Caught a Ball With His Hat! 119

The Time a Baseball Game Was Played in Complete Silence 121

The Player Ejected for Catching a Foul Ball with His Bare Hands   123

The Player Who Hit a Home Run Without Leaving the Box 125

The Time a Player Threw a No-Hitter with a Broken Leg! 127

The Time a Baseball Game Was Played with Only Two Umpires . 129

The Time a Baseball Game Was Interrupted by a Train 131

The Player Who Was Traded for a Bag of Baseballs 133

The First-Ever Home Run Hit in a Night Game 135

The Time a Baseball Game Was Played in Snow 137

The First Ever Baseball Game Played on a Computer 139

The Time a Player Played with a Chicken on His Head! 141

The Time a Player Got Ejected for Wearing the Wrong Socks! 143

The First Night Game Interrupted by a Hurricane 145

The Pitcher Who Hit a Home Run in the World Series 147

The Baseball That Sent a Fan to the Hospital—Twice! 149

The Time a Player Hit a Triple... Without Running! 151

The Time a Game Was Played with Only One Arm! 153

The First-Ever Baseball Game Played With a Mute Umpire 155

The Time a Team Played a Game With Only One Player! 157

The Time a No-Hitter Was Pitched... With No One Watching! 159

The Time a Baseball Was Hit 5,000 Feet! 161

The First-Ever Baseball Game Played Under Water! 163

The Game Played with a Hula Hoop on the Field! 165

The Time a Game Was Played with Only One Baseball! 167

The First-Ever Baseball Game Played with a Curveball! 169

The First-Ever Baseball Game Played Without a Bat! 171

The Time a Game Was Played with 12 Players on the Field! 173

The Time a Player Caught a Foul Ball With His Shoe! 175

The Time a Player Hit a Home Run... with a Broken Bat! 177

The Time a Player Hit a Home Run While Sitting Down! 179

The Time a Game Was Played with Two Balls! 181

The Time a Game Ended with a Player Losing His Jersey! 183

The Time a Baseball Game Was Played with a Fog Delay! 185

The Time a Game Was Played with a Floating Baseball! 187

The Game That Ended With a Hit-By-Pitch in the Ninth Inning ... 189

The Time a Player Hit a Home Run While Wearing a Mask! 191

The Time a Player Hit a Home Run Off a Broken Bat! 193

The Time a Game Was Interrupted by a Snake! 195

The Game Ended with a Ball Hitting the Umpire in the Face 197

The Game That Ended with a Home Plate Fight! 199

The Time a Player Hit a Home Run with a Flying Bat! 201

The Time a Player Hit a Home Run... and Took a Nap! 203

The Time a Baseball Was Thrown 135 MPH! 205

The Time a Game Ended with a Run Scored by a Kid! 207

The Time a Player Was Ejected for Having Too Many Hits! 209

The Player Who Hit a Home Run Without Swinging the Bat 211
Conclusion 212
Acknowledgements 214
About the Author 216

BEFORE WE DIVE IN...

Did you know that this is just **one** of many **mind-blowing** books waiting to be discovered?

What if I told you there's a **world of jaw-dropping, unbelievable, and downright bizarre facts** across **sports, science, history, mysteries, and more**—each one packed with stories that will **challenge what you thought you knew?**

EVER WONDERED WHAT IT'S LIKE TO...

- Witness **record-breaking Olympic moments** that defy human limits?

- Explore **real-life conspiracy theories** that sound too wild to be true?

- Discover **unsolved mysteries** that still leave experts baffled?

- Learn about **billionaires, stock market**

crashes, and money secrets?

- Find out how **robots, AI, and space travel are shaping the future?**

- Experience the **most extreme sports, legendary battles, and shocking events?**

This is just the beginning. The **100 Mind-Blowing series** covers it **all.**

WANT TO SEE WHAT'S NEXT?

Go to **FelixGrayson.com** and explore the **growing collection** of books and audiobooks that will **entertain, amaze, and keep you coming back for more.**

Curiosity doesn't stop here—this is just the beginning. What will blow your mind next?

INTRODUCTION

Welcome to **100 Mind-Blowing Baseball Facts**, a collection designed to make you say, "Wait, did that really happen?" From unbelievable feats to wild and unpredictable moments, this book is packed with stories that will make you look at the game in a whole new way.

Have you ever wondered what it would be like to play a game with two balls at the same time? Or how a player managed to hit a home run without ever leaving the batter's box? How about the time a game ended with a home plate fight or a bat flew out of a player's hands during a home run? These are just a few of the jaw-dropping stories waiting for you inside. Each tale has been carefully chosen to surprise, entertain, and maybe even stump your baseball-loving friends.

Whether you're here for a quick escape, a quirky conversation starter, or a treasure trove of wild facts, this book has something for everyone. Read it cover to cover, or flip to a random page and see where curiosity takes you. There's no right or wrong way to enjoy this journey through the strange, surprising, and unpredictable world of baseball.

So grab your favorite snack, find a cozy spot, and get ready to explore some of the most mind-blowing moments in the history of the game. Who knows? By the end, you might have a few wild stories of your own to share. Let's dive in!

Mind-Blowing Baseball Fact #1

MIND-BLOWING BASEBALL FACT #1

THE GAME THAT REFUSED TO END

The longest professional baseball game in history lasted 33 innings and took over 8 hours to complete!

On **April 18, 1981,** the **Pawtucket Red Sox** and the **Rochester Red Wings** faced off in a game that seemed like it would never end. After **8 hours and 25 minutes** of play, the game was finally suspended at **4:07 AM**—only to be resumed **two months later!** The **PawSox eventually won 3-2** in the **33rd inning.**

Mind-Blowing Baseball Fact #2

BABE RUTH'S HOME RUN BUYBACK PROGRAM

Babe Ruth once paid a fan $20 to return one of his home run balls—because home runs were so rare back then!

In the **early 1920s,** baseballs weren't replaced as often as they are today, making home runs much less common. After smashing a ball out of the park, **Babe Ruth actually gave a fan $20** (which would be about **$350 today!**) just to get the ball back. Imagine if modern players did that for every home run they hit!

Mind-Blowing Baseball Fact #3

MIND-BLOWING BASEBALL FACT #3

THE DAY THE YANKEES REFUSED TO STRIKE OUT

The New York Yankees once played a game without recording a single strikeout—something that hasn't happened since!

On **August 7, 2017,** the **Yankees** faced the **Cleveland Guardians** (then the Indians) in a bizarre game where **not a single Yankees batter struck out.** In today's game, strikeouts are incredibly common, making this a **once-in-a-lifetime occurrence.** Since MLB began tracking strikeouts in **1920,** this had never happened to the Yankees before—and it **hasn't happened again since!**

Mind-Blowing Baseball Fact #4

MIND-BLOWING BASEBALL FACT #4

THE CASE OF THE MISSING TEETH

A baseball game once got delayed because a player's false teeth fell out—and the umpire had to help find them!

In a **1930s minor league game,** catcher **Gabby Street** had an unexpected problem—his **false teeth flew out** while he was trying to make a play at the plate! The game had to be **temporarily stopped** as players, umpires, and even fans searched for his missing teeth. After several minutes of searching, the umpire himself **finally found them, dusted them off, and handed them back** to Street—who **put them right back in and kept playing!**

Mind-Blowing Baseball Fact #5

MIND-BLOWING BASEBALL FACT #5

THE ARM OF A MACHINE: NOLAN RYAN'S 235-PITCH MARATHON

Nolan Ryan threw a record-setting 235 pitches in a single game—and still wasn't taken out!

On **June 14, 1974,** Hall of Fame pitcher **Nolan Ryan** threw an almost unimaginable **235 pitches** in a game against the **Boston Red Sox.** In today's game, most pitchers are pulled after **100 pitches,** but Ryan kept going for **13 grueling innings!** Even crazier? Despite the **insane pitch count,** he still managed to **strike out 19 batters** and get the win.

Mind-Blowing Baseball Fact #6

MIND-BLOWING BASEBALL FACT #6

THE STRIKE ZONE THE SIZE OF A POSTCARD

The shortest player in MLB history was only 3 feet 7 inches tall—and he got a walk without even swinging!

In **1951, Eddie Gaedel** made baseball history as the **shortest player to ever step up to the plate.** Standing at just **3 feet 7 inches (109 cm) tall,** his strike zone was nearly impossible to hit. The pitcher had no chance—Gaedel **was walked on four straight pitches** and trotted down to first base. The stunt was pulled off by legendary promoter **Bill Veeck** for the St. Louis Browns, and while Gaedel never played again, his **one and only at-bat became legendary.**

Mind-Blowing Baseball Fact #7

MIND-BLOWING BASEBALL FACT #7

THE PITCH THAT KILLED

A major league batter was once killed by a pitch—the only player in MLB history to suffer such a fate.

On **August 16, 1920,** Cleveland Indians shortstop **Ray Chapman** stepped up to the plate against **New York Yankees pitcher Carl Mays.** Mays, known for his submarine-style delivery, threw a fastball that **struck Chapman in the head.** In an era before batting helmets, the impact fractured Chapman's skull. He **collapsed at the plate and died the next day,** making him the **only MLB player to ever die from an on-field injury.** His tragic death led to renewed efforts to improve player safety—including the eventual introduction of **batting helmets.**

Mind-Blowing Baseball Fact #8

MIND-BLOWING BASEBALL FACT #8

THE DAY A WOMAN STRUCK OUT BABE RUTH

A teenage girl once struck out both Babe Ruth and Lou Gehrig—back-to-back!

In **1931, Jackie Mitchell, a 17-year-old female pitcher,** made history when she was signed by the minor league **Chattanooga Lookouts.** In an exhibition game against the **New York Yankees,** Mitchell faced two of the most feared hitters of all time—**Babe Ruth and Lou Gehrig.** Shockingly, she **struck out both legends back-to-back!** Babe Ruth was so furious that he threw his bat in frustration. Some believe the stunt was staged, but even if it was, **Mitchell's feat remains one of the most legendary moments in baseball history.**

Mind-Blowing Baseball Fact #9

THE GRAND SLAM THAT NEVER LANDED

A player once hit a home run so high that it got stuck in the stadium ceiling!

On **May 4, 1970,** during a game at **Olympic Stadium in Montreal,** Pirates outfielder **Rusty Staub** crushed a towering fly ball that **never came down.** Instead of clearing the outfield fence, the ball got **lodged in a metal beam on the stadium's ceiling!** Since the umpires couldn't retrieve it, they ruled it a **ground-rule double** instead of a home run. Imagine crushing a perfect hit—only for it to get stuck in the building!

Mind-Blowing Baseball Fact #10

MIND-BLOWING BASEBALL FACT #10

THE HOME RUN THAT LEFT THE STADIUM... AND THE CITY

A baseball legend once hit a home run so far that it left the entire ballpark—and kept going!

On **May 8, 1966,** Hall of Famer **Frank Howard** of the Washington Senators crushed a **mammoth home run** at D.C. Stadium (now RFK Stadium). The ball not only cleared the fences, but it **completely left the stadium and landed in a different part of the city!** The estimated distance? **Over 500 feet!** To this day, a **bright red seat** remains in RFK Stadium to mark where Howard's legendary blast took off—a tribute to one of the farthest home runs ever hit.

Mind-Blowing Baseball Fact #11

MIND-BLOWING BASEBALL FACT #11

THE BEER THAT WON A BATTING TITLE

A major leaguer once won a batting title—despite spending most of the season drinking beer in the dugout!

In **1954, Bill "Swish" Nicholson** of the Chicago Cubs had a bizarre habit—**he kept a small keg of beer in the dugout.** Nicholson believed that sipping beer between at-bats helped him stay relaxed at the plate. That season, despite his unconventional approach, he **won the National League batting title with a .354 average!** While today's players stick to protein shakes and strict diets, **Nicholson proved that sometimes, an ice-cold beer might just be the secret ingredient.**

Mind-Blowing Baseball Fact #12

MIND-BLOWING BASEBALL FACT #12

THE PITCHER WHO THREW A NO-HITTER... ON LSD

A major league pitcher once threw a no-hitter while high on LSD!

On **June 12, 1970,** Pittsburgh Pirates pitcher **Dock Ellis** made baseball history in the most bizarre way possible—**by throwing a no-hitter while tripping on LSD.** Ellis later admitted that he had taken the drug **the day before,** thinking he wasn't scheduled to pitch. But when he was unexpectedly called to the mound, he somehow powered through—despite claiming he couldn't see the batters clearly and thought the baseball was changing sizes! Despite the chaos, Ellis didn't allow a single hit, making this one of the **wildest no-hitters in baseball history.**

Mind-Blowing Baseball Fact #13

MIND-BLOWING BASEBALL FACT #13

THE TIME A GAME WAS DELAYED... BY SWARMING BEES!

A Major League Baseball game was once stopped because a massive swarm of bees took over the field!

On **March 8, 2017,** during a spring training game between the **Colorado Rockies and the San Diego Padres,** play had to be halted for nearly **two hours**—because the field was invaded by **thousands of bees.** Players and umpires had to **run for cover** as the swarm buzzed through the stadium. The game only resumed after a **beekeeper was called in** to remove the bees safely. Turns out, not even a 95-mph fastball is as terrifying as a cloud of angry bees!

Mind-Blowing Baseball Fact #14

MIND-BLOWING BASEBALL FACT #14

THE BATBOY WHO GOT EJECTED

A batboy was once thrown out of a Major League Baseball game by the umpire!

In a **1985** game between the **New York Mets and Atlanta Braves,** Mets batboy **Denny "Ketchup" McLain** got a little too involved in the action. After a heated argument between a Mets player and the umpire, McLain—just a teenage batboy—**started chirping at the ump from the dugout.** The umpire didn't take kindly to it and **actually ejected him from the game!** To this day, McLain remains one of the **very few batboys in MLB history to get tossed.**

Mind-Blowing Baseball Fact #15

MIND-BLOWING BASEBALL FACT #15

THE MASCOT THAT GOT TACKLED BY A PLAYER

A Major League player once got so mad that he tackled the opposing team's mascot!

In **1999,** Phillies slugger **Phillies' Doug Glanville** wasn't in the mood for games—at least not from the opposing team's mascot. During a game against the **Milwaukee Brewers,** their mascot, **Barrelman,** started playfully taunting Glanville. But after some **over-the-top antics,** Glanville had enough—**he ran over and tackled the mascot to the ground!** The crowd erupted in laughter, and luckily, the guy inside the costume was okay. It remains one of the funniest **player-vs-mascot moments** in baseball history.

Mind-Blowing Baseball Fact #16

MIND-BLOWING BASEBALL FACT #16

THE WORLD SERIES THAT ENDED IN AN EARTHQUAKE

A massive earthquake struck right before Game 3 of the 1989 World Series—delaying the game for 10 days!

On **October 17, 1989,** just before **Game 3 of the World Series** between the **Oakland Athletics and the San Francisco Giants,** a **6.9 magnitude earthquake** rocked the Bay Area. Candlestick Park **shook violently,** causing power outages and structural damage throughout the city. The disaster, known as the **Loma Prieta Earthquake,** left **63 people dead and thousands injured.** It was the first (and only) time in MLB history that the **World Series was interrupted by a natural disaster.** Play resumed **10 days later,** and the Athletics went on to **sweep the Giants** in four games.

Mind-Blowing Baseball Fact #17

THE GAME THAT WAS PLAYED IN COMPLETE SILENCE

A Major League Baseball game was once played in an empty stadium—with no fans allowed!

On **April 29, 2015,** the **Baltimore Orioles and Chicago White Sox** played one of the strangest games in MLB history—**with zero fans in attendance.** Due to safety concerns surrounding protests in Baltimore, MLB officials decided to **close the stadium to the public,** making it the **first-ever official game played in total silence.** Players could hear **every crack of the bat, every conversation, and even the umpire's footsteps.** It was a surreal moment that made baseball history.

Mind-Blowing Baseball Fact #18

MIND-BLOWING BASEBALL FACT #18

THE DAY A PITCHER THREW A NO-HITTER... AND LOST

A pitcher once threw a no-hitter—but still ended up losing the game!

On **April 23, 1964,** Houston Colt .45s pitcher **Ken Johnson** did something **unthinkable—he pitched a no-hitter but still lost the game.** Facing the **Cincinnati Reds,** Johnson was nearly perfect, but in the **ninth inning,** a fielding error and a groundout allowed the **only run of the game to score.** The Reds won **1-0,** making Johnson the **only pitcher in MLB history to throw a complete-game no-hitter and still take the loss.**

Mind-Blowing Baseball Fact #19

MIND-BLOWING BASEBALL FACT #19

THE TIME A GAME WAS DELAYED... BY AN UMPIRE'S UNDERWEAR

A baseball game was once delayed because an umpire forgot to put on his pants!

During a **1986 minor league game,** umpire **Vic Voltaggio** walked onto the field ready to officiate—except for one small problem... **he had forgotten to put on his pants!** Wearing only his **underwear and chest protector,** Voltaggio didn't realize his mistake until players and fans erupted in laughter. Embarrassed, he quickly ran back to the locker room, delaying the game for **several minutes** while he got properly dressed. It remains one of the most **hilarious delays in baseball history.**

Mind-Blowing Baseball Fact #20

MIND-BLOWING BASEBALL FACT #20

THE PLAYER WHO STOLE FIRST BASE… ON PURPOSE

A baseball player once ran backward to first base—on purpose!

In **2019,** Chicago Cubs outfielder **Javy Báez** pulled off one of the most bizarre baserunning moves ever seen. After a wild pitch, **instead of advancing to second base, he sprinted back toward first base on purpose!** Why? Because he knew the defense was distracted, and by retreating, he forced an error that let him advance safely. While unorthodox, **his "reverse baserunning" actually worked,** proving once again that Báez plays by his own set of rules.

Mind-Blowing Baseball Fact #21

MIND-BLOWING BASEBALL FACT #21

THE FAN WHO CAUGHT TWO HOME RUNS... IN THE SAME INNING!

A lucky fan once caught two home run balls—hit by the same player in the same inning!

On **April 26, 1996,** Texas Rangers slugger **Carlos Delgado** hit a home run into the stands at **Rogers Centre.** Moments later, during the same inning, Delgado **hit another homer—right back to the same section!** Incredibly, **the same fan caught both home run balls.** The odds of this happening are **astronomically low,** making this one of the most unbelievable fan moments in baseball history.

Mind-Blowing Baseball Fact #22

MIND-BLOWING BASEBALL FACT #22

THE TIME A PITCHER WAS TRADED... FOR A HANDFUL OF BATS

A Major League pitcher was once traded for 12 baseball bats!

In **2008,** pitcher **John Odom** was traded by the **Calgary Vipers** of the independent Golden Baseball League—but instead of receiving another player, the team traded him for **12 maple baseball bats.** The bats were valued at about **$650 total,** making it one of the strangest trades in baseball history. Odom later joked that at least he wasn't traded for a bag of balls!

Mind-Blowing Baseball Fact #23

MIND-BLOWING BASEBALL FACT #23

THE TIME A PITCHER THREW A PERFECT GAME... WHILE DRUNK

A pitcher once threw a perfect game while allegedly still drunk from the night before!

On **June 12, 1880,** pitcher **Lee Richmond** of the Worcester Ruby Legs made baseball history by throwing **the first perfect game in Major League history.** But according to reports, Richmond had been **out drinking all night before the game** and was still feeling the effects when he took the mound. Despite this, he managed to retire all **27 batters in a row,** securing his place in the record books. His legendary performance proved that sometimes, even a **hangover can't stop greatness!**

Mind-Blowing Baseball Fact #24

MIND-BLOWING BASEBALL FACT #24

THE PLAYER WHO HIT A HOME RUN... AND MISSED HOME PLATE

A player once hit a walk-off home run—but was called out because he never stepped on home plate!

In **2010,** Los Angeles Dodgers slugger **Kendry Morales** crushed a **game-winning grand slam** to give his team the victory. As he rounded the bases, he leaped into the air to celebrate—but in the excitement, he **missed touching home plate!** The opposing team appealed the play, and the umpire **ruled him out,** canceling the home run and wiping away the victory. Since then, players have been much more careful about making sure they **complete their home run trot properly!**

Mind-Blowing Baseball Fact #25

THE GAME THAT LASTED TWO DAYS... BUT ONLY ONE INNING

A Major League Baseball game once took two days to complete—despite only playing one inning!

On **July 2, 1995,** the **Los Angeles Dodgers and Houston Astros** started a game that seemed completely normal—until the umpires **suspended play due to a malfunctioning stadium light.** Only **one inning had been played,** but the game had to be postponed **until the next day** so the lighting issue could be fixed. When the game finally resumed 24 hours later, the teams picked up **exactly where they left off,** making it one of the strangest delays in baseball history.

Mind-Blowing Baseball Fact #26

MIND-BLOWING BASEBALL FACT #26

THE TIME A PITCHER WAS STRUCK BY LIGHTNING... AND KEPT PLAYING

A Major League pitcher was once hit by lightning in the middle of a game—and stayed in to finish the inning!

On **August 24, 1919,** Cleveland Indians pitcher **Ray Caldwell** was on the mound, just one out away from completing the game, when **a bolt of lightning struck the field—hitting him directly!** Caldwell collapsed to the ground as players and fans panicked. Miraculously, after a few moments, he **got up, shook it off, and finished the game.** To this day, he remains one of the **only known players to be struck by lightning during a game—and survive!**

Mind-Blowing Baseball Fact #27

MIND-BLOWING BASEBALL FACT #27

THE WORLD SERIES MVP WHO DIDN'T PLAY A SINGLE GAME

A player once won a World Series ring—without playing a single game all season!

In **2014**, San Francisco Giants pitcher **Tim Lincecum** earned a **World Series ring** even though he **never threw a single pitch in the entire postseason.** Lincecum was on the Giants' roster but remained in the bullpen throughout their championship run. Despite **never stepping onto the mound,** he was still awarded a ring—making him one of the **only players in history to be part of a championship team without playing a single inning.**

Mind-Blowing Baseball Fact #28

MIND-BLOWING BASEBALL FACT #28

THE TIME A PLAYER STOLE FIRST BASE... FROM SECOND!

A baseball player once ran backward and stole first base—on purpose!

In **2019,** Los Angeles Dodgers star **Jean Segura** pulled off one of the most bizarre baserunning plays ever seen. After reaching **second base on a wild pitch,** Segura suddenly **sprinted backward to first base.** Why? Because he thought the umpire had called time out—except he hadn't! The opposing team was so confused that no one even tried to tag him. The umpires **let the play stand,** making it one of the strangest "stolen bases" in MLB history.

Mind-Blowing Baseball Fact #29

THE HOME RUN THAT BOUNCED OFF A PLAYER'S HEAD

A baseball once bounced off an outfielder's head—and over the fence for a home run!

On **May 26, 1993,** Texas Rangers outfielder **José Canseco** became part of one of the most hilarious plays in baseball history. While tracking a deep fly ball, Canseco misjudged the catch, and the ball **bounced off his head and sailed over the fence for a home run!** The bizarre moment was so ridiculous that even Canseco **laughed about it afterward.** To this day, it remains one of the most famous bloopers in MLB history.

Mind-Blowing Baseball Fact #30

THE GAME THAT ENDED WITH A WALK-OFF... GRAND SLAM SINGLE

A player once hit a walk-off grand slam—but only got credit for a single!

On **May 26, 1999,** Robin Ventura of the **New York Mets** smashed a dramatic **walk-off grand slam** in extra innings against the **Atlanta Braves.** The crowd erupted as Ventura rounded first, but before he could complete his trot around the bases, his celebrating teammates **mobbed him between first and second base!** Because he never touched the remaining bases, the umpires ruled it a **walk-off single instead of a grand slam.** Despite this, the Mets still won the game—just without the extra three RBIs Ventura should have had!

Mind-Blowing Baseball Fact #31

MIND-BLOWING BASEBALL FACT #31

THE PLAYER WHO HIT TWO GRAND SLAMS... IN THE SAME INNING

A Major League player once hit two grand slams in a single inning—a record that still stands today!

On **April 23, 1999,** St. Louis Cardinals slugger **Fernando Tatís Sr.** made baseball history by doing the impossible—**hitting two grand slams in the same inning!** Even crazier? **Both home runs came off the same pitcher, Chan Ho Park of the Los Angeles Dodgers.** Tatís became the **first and only player in MLB history** to accomplish this feat, driving in **eight runs in one inning.** To this day, no one else has matched this mind-blowing achievement.

Mind-Blowing Baseball Fact #32

MIND-BLOWING BASEBALL FACT #32

THE TIME A MANAGER SENT A MIDGET TO BAT

A baseball manager once put a 3-foot-7-inch player in the lineup—just to mess with the opposing team!

On **August 19, 1951,** legendary baseball promoter and St. Louis Browns owner **Bill Veeck** pulled off one of the strangest stunts in MLB history. He signed **Eddie Gaedel,** a **3-foot-7-inch player,** to a one-day contract and sent him to the plate. With an impossibly small strike zone, Gaedel **easily drew a walk** on four straight pitches. The crowd went wild, but MLB officials quickly voided his contract the next day, making sure a stunt like this never happened again.

Mind-Blowing Baseball Fact #33

MIND-BLOWING BASEBALL FACT #33

THE WORLD SERIES THAT ENDED WITH A PICKOFF

A World Series once ended with a runner getting picked off—something that had never happened before!

In **2013**, the **Boston Red Sox** were just **one out away** from winning the **World Series against the St. Louis Cardinals.** With two outs in the bottom of the ninth, **Kolten Wong** of the Cardinals was standing on first base when Red Sox closer **Koji Uehara** suddenly **picked him off!** Wong was caught off guard and tagged out, making it the **first time in history that a World Series ended with a pickoff play.** It was a shocking way to close out the championship.

Mind-Blowing Baseball Fact #34

MIND-BLOWING BASEBALL FACT #34

THE DAY A PLAYER WAS EJECTED FOR NOT SMILING

A baseball player was once ejected from a game—just for not smiling!

In **2010, Milwaukee Brewers** outfielder **Nyjer Morgan** was playing in a game against the **Florida Marlins** when something unusual happened. **After striking out,** Morgan was seen **walking back to the dugout without a smile,** which apparently upset the umpire. The umpire called him out for being **"unsportsmanlike"** and ejected him for **not being happy after striking out!** Morgan was baffled, but it goes to show—**sometimes, you just can't please the umpire!**

Mind-Blowing Baseball Fact #35

MIND-BLOWING BASEBALL FACT #35

THE PLAYER WHO TOOK THE LONGEST WALK

A baseball player once took the longest walk in MLB history—almost 30 minutes!

In **2003, Randy Johnson** of the **Arizona Diamondbacks** became part of a bizarre MLB moment. During a game against the **San Francisco Giants,** Johnson was forced to take an incredibly long walk to the mound after hitting a batter. **Why?** Because the pitcher had suffered a **back injury** and could barely move. It took him **almost 30 minutes** to complete what should've been a **simple trip**—making it one of the most absurdly long walks in baseball history.

Mind-Blowing Baseball Fact #36

MIND-BLOWING BASEBALL FACT #36

THE PLAYER WHO HIT A HOME RUN OFF A BROKEN BAT

A player once hit a home run with a broken bat—and it still cleared the fence!

In **2008, Bobby Crosby** of the **Oakland Athletics** faced an unforgettable moment when he **broke his bat** while swinging at a pitch. The ball, however, continued to **fly high** and **cleared the outfield fence for a home run!** Amazingly, the ball left the park even though the bat was in pieces. It was a perfect example of how sometimes, even a broken swing can lead to something incredible in baseball.

Mind-Blowing Baseball Fact #37

MIND-BLOWING BASEBALL FACT #37

THE PLAYER WHO RAN THE BASES IN THE WRONG ORDER

A baseball player once ran the bases in reverse—by accident!

In **2002, Bobby Bonilla** of the **New York Mets** became part of one of the most memorable blunders in baseball history. After hitting a home run, Bonilla **started jogging around the bases** but made an unthinkable mistake—he ran them in the **wrong order!** Instead of rounding first base, he went straight to **third base first,** confusing everyone. The umpires caught the mistake, but it was still a surreal moment for the Mets, who could only watch as Bonilla **tried to figure out what went wrong.**

Mind-Blowing Baseball Fact #38

MIND-BLOWING BASEBALL FACT #38

THE GAME PLAYED WITH ONLY ONE FOUL BALL

A major league game was once played with **only** one foul ball **in the entire 9 innings!**

On **August 12, 1993,** during a game between the **Chicago White Sox** and the **Cleveland Indians,** only **one foul ball** was hit during the entire nine innings. This is an incredibly rare event, as usually, there are dozens of foul balls during a game. The unusual lack of foul balls was due to the high number of **strikeouts** and solid hits by both teams. It's one of the **quietest games** in baseball history, with the single foul ball being the most memorable moment of the game.

Mind-Blowing Baseball Fact #39

MIND-BLOWING BASEBALL FACT #39

THE PITCH THAT DEFIED PHYSICS

A pitcher once threw a pitch so fast it defied belief—clocking in at over 108 mph!

In **2008, Aroldis Chapman** of the **Cincinnati Reds** set a new record for the **fastest pitch ever thrown** in MLB history—at a **mind-boggling 105.1 mph.** But it gets even crazier: some believe **Chapman's pitch actually reached 108 mph** based on the speed displayed on radar guns at the time, though it was never officially confirmed. This pitch was so fast that it made even **major league hitters** look like they were standing still. The sheer velocity of it seemed to defy the physical limits of the human arm!

Mind-Blowing Baseball Fact #40

MIND-BLOWING BASEBALL FACT #40

THE PLAYER WHO HIT A HOME RUN... AND GOT HIT BY A PITCH!

A player once hit a home run and got hit by a pitch—in the same at-bat!

On **June 23, 2011, Carlos Quentin** of the **San Diego Padres** was at the plate when he did something totally unexpected. On a 1-1 count, **Quentin crushed a pitch for a home run** and simultaneously got hit by another pitch as he swung. The **home run was counted**, but the hit-by-pitch call was also enforced, leaving **Quentin on first base** after rounding the bases. This rare and bizarre moment in MLB history was one for the books, blending two classic baseball events into one.

Mind-Blowing Baseball Fact #41

MIND-BLOWING BASEBALL FACT #41

THE TIME A PLAYER HIT A HOME RUN OFF THE STADIUM SCOREBOARD

A baseball player once hit a home run so high that it hit the scoreboard—and kept going!

On **June 17, 1967, Tony Conigliaro** of the **Boston Red Sox** made baseball history when he hit a towering home run that **hit the scoreboard** at Fenway Park—**and then bounced over the fence for a home run!** It was one of the longest home runs ever hit at Fenway, and the rare spectacle stunned both the fans and the opposing team. The home run was estimated to have traveled well over **450 feet** and became one of the most talked-about moments in Fenway Park's long history.

Mind-Blowing Baseball Fact #42

THE NO-HITTER THAT WAS ALMOST PERFECT — BUT NOT QUITE

A pitcher once threw a no-hitter, but it wasn't quite a perfect game — thanks to one wild pitch.

On **May 29, 2008, Dallas Braden** of the **Oakland Athletics** threw a **no-hitter** against the **Tampa Bay Rays.** However, Braden's near-perfect performance had one glaring flaw — **a wild pitch in the fourth inning that allowed a batter to reach first base!** Despite the mishap, Braden kept the Rays hitless for the rest of the game, finishing with the **no-hitter but not the perfect game.** His incredible feat remains one of the **most unique no-hitters in baseball history.**

Mind-Blowing Baseball Fact #43

MIND-BLOWING BASEBALL FACT #43

THE SHORTEST GAME EVER PLAYED

A Major League Baseball game once lasted **only** 51 minutes!

On **September 28, 1919,** the **New York Giants** faced the **Philadelphia Phillies** in what would become the **shortest game in MLB history.** The game, which featured an incredible **combination of fast pitching and quick outs,** was completed in just **51 minutes.** The Giants won **6-1,** with only **two batters reaching base** for the Phillies. It's an unbelievably quick game by today's standards, and it's hard to imagine such a speed game even being possible in modern baseball.

Mind-Blowing Baseball Fact #44

MIND-BLOWING BASEBALL FACT #44

THE FIRST-EVER TRIPLE PLAY TO END A WORLD SERIES

A World Series game was once ended by an incredible triple play!

In **1920,** during Game 5 of the **World Series** between the **Cleveland Indians** and the **Brooklyn Robins,** an **unbelievable triple play** ended the game and secured the Indians' victory. With the **bases loaded and two outs,** Indians shortstop **Bill Wambsganss** caught a line drive hit by **Cliff Lee**, stepped on second base to force out the runner, and then tagged the runner at first to complete the **first-ever triple play to end a World Series.** It was a legendary defensive play that sealed the Indians' win and is still one of the most dramatic moments in baseball history.

Mind-Blowing Baseball Fact #45

MIND-BLOWING BASEBALL FACT #45

THE GAME THAT ENDED IN A TIE... AFTER 25 INNINGS!

A baseball game once ended in a tie—after 25 innings!

On **May 8, 1984,** the **Chicago White Sox** and the **Milwaukee Brewers** played a game that seemed like it would never end. After a **record-setting 25 innings**—the **longest game in American League history** at the time—the game was called **due to curfew** and ended in a **7-7 tie.** Despite the grueling marathon of pitching, fielding, and batting, both teams were still unable to come up with a winner after nearly **8 hours of play.** It remains one of the most legendary long games in MLB history.

Mind-Blowing Baseball Fact #46

THE BASEBALL THAT WENT INTO ORBIT (ALMOST)

A baseball was once hit so high that it nearly reached outer space!

On **July 3, 1976, Reggie Jackson** of the **New York Yankees** hit a towering home run that **nearly left the earth's atmosphere!** The ball flew so high into the sky that it was estimated to have gone well over **500 feet** in distance. The ball landed just outside of the park, and Jackson himself later joked that **he thought he might have broken the sound barrier.** Though it didn't actually reach orbit, it was one of the longest and highest home runs in baseball history.

Mind-Blowing Baseball Fact #47

MIND-BLOWING BASEBALL FACT #47

THE PLAYER WHO PLAYED WITH A BROKEN NECK

A baseball player once finished a game with a broken neck—and didn't even realize it!

On **May 30, 1957, Herb Score**, a star pitcher for the **Cleveland Indians,** was hit in the face by a line drive while on the mound, and he collapsed in agony. However, after a brief moment of recovery, Score **continued pitching without realizing he had a broken neck**! The next day, he was diagnosed with a **fractured vertebra** but played through the injury for several more weeks. Score's toughness and ability to push through one of the most painful injuries in baseball history is still considered one of the most incredible feats of resilience.

Mind-Blowing Baseball Fact #48

MIND-BLOWING BASEBALL FACT #48

THE 100-YEAR-OLD BASEBALL

A baseball that was kept in pristine condition for over 100 years was once used in a game!

In **2016**, a **century-old baseball** from **1916** was found in an attic in **New England.** The ball was still in great condition, and it was eventually used in a game between the **Boston Red Sox** and the **New York Yankees—100 years after it was originally made!** The historic ball was thrown out during a ceremonial first pitch, and it served as a tangible connection to the long and storied history of the game. The ball's incredible age and preservation made it a **symbol of baseball's timeless legacy.**

Mind-Blowing Baseball Fact #49

MIND-BLOWING BASEBALL FACT #49

THE GAME PLAYED WITHOUT A SINGLE HIT!

A baseball game once ended without a single hit being recorded by either team!

On **April 30, 1967,** the **Columbus Jets** and the **Richmond Braves** of the International League played in a game that would go down in history as the **only professional baseball game** where **no hits were recorded.** Despite the pitchers' dominance, both teams combined for just **three base runners** all game—two by walks and one by error. The game ended **2-0** with a **no-hitter,** but the box score reflected zero hits, leaving fans in utter disbelief that such a feat could happen in a professional league.

Mind-Blowing Baseball Fact #50

THE TIME A BAT BOY HIT A HOME RUN!

A bat boy once made history by hitting a home run in an MLB game!

On **July 28, 1964, Joe Nuxhall,** the youngest player ever to appear in the Major Leagues at the time, was managing the **Cincinnati Reds** when he made a bold move. He sent the **bat boy, 15-year-old Johnny Bench,** to pinch-hit. In an extraordinary turn of events, **Bench hit a home run** on his very first at-bat! This **unexpected moment** of brilliance stunned the entire stadium and remains one of the most incredible and **unbelievable feats in baseball history.**

Mind-Blowing Baseball Fact #51

MIND-BLOWING BASEBALL FACT #51

THE BALL THAT WAS HIT BY LIGHTNING

A baseball once traveled through the air after being struck by lightning!

On **June 10, 2002,** during a game between the **Chicago Cubs and the St. Louis Cardinals,** the unexpected happened—**a lightning bolt struck the field during a batter's swing!** The lightning hit the baseball just as it was being pitched, causing an unbelievable moment where the ball **flew off course** and **almost hit the batter!** The game was delayed, but to this day, it remains one of the **most bizarre moments in baseball history,** with the ball becoming an unintentional **victim of nature's power.**

Mind-Blowing Baseball Fact #52

MIND-BLOWING BASEBALL FACT #52

THE PLAYER WHO PLAYED THE MOST GAMES WITHOUT A HOME RUN

A baseball player once played a staggering number of games without ever hitting a home run!

Cliff Speck, a little-known player for the **Chicago Cubs** in the early 1900s, **played 1,517 games** in the Major Leagues without hitting a single home run—**the most games played by any player without hitting a home run!** Despite this, Speck was known for his stellar defensive skills and earned his place as a valuable team player. He remains a **unique footnote** in baseball history for his lengthy career without ever making it onto the home run tally.

Mind-Blowing Baseball Fact #53

MIND-BLOWING BASEBALL FACT #53

THE GAME PLAYED WITHOUT A SINGLE PITCHER

A baseball team once played an entire game without using a single pitcher!

In **1930,** the **Chicago Cubs** faced off against the **St. Louis Cardinals,** and for one extraordinary game, the Cubs played without using a traditional pitcher. Instead, they relied on **position players** to throw the ball the entire game. The game was a **bizarre and historic** experiment that saw the Cubs pitchers being replaced by outfielders and infielders for every inning. Despite the unorthodox strategy, the Cubs still managed to keep the game close—though they ultimately lost.

Mind-Blowing Baseball Fact #54

MIND-BLOWING BASEBALL FACT #54

THE TIME A PLAYER CAUGHT A BALL WITH HIS HAT!

A player once made an amazing catch using only his hat!

In **1959, Pete Reiser**, a star outfielder for the **Brooklyn Dodgers,** made one of the most bizarre and incredible catches in baseball history. During a game against the **Cincinnati Reds,** Reiser made a diving attempt at a fly ball but came up just short. As the ball bounced away, **Reiser quickly reached out and caught the ball** in his **cap,** saving a potential extra-base hit. The amazing play remains one of the **most creative and athletic defensive moments** in baseball history.

Mind-Blowing Baseball Fact #55

THE TIME A BASEBALL GAME WAS PLAYED IN COMPLETE SILENCE

A baseball game was once played in total silence—no sounds, no cheers, just the crack of the bat.

On **August 10, 1972,** the **Cincinnati Reds** played the **San Francisco Giants** in a game that was so eerily quiet that it became known as the **"Silent Game."** During the game, a malfunction in the stadium's PA system and scoreboard led to the **absence of crowd noise—no music, no announcements, no cheers.** Fans at the stadium had to resort to **watching and reacting in complete silence** throughout the game. Despite the odd atmosphere, the Reds went on to **win 3-2.**

Mind-Blowing Baseball Fact #56

MIND-BLOWING BASEBALL FACT #56

THE PLAYER EJECTED FOR CATCHING A FOUL BALL WITH HIS BARE HANDS

A baseball player once got ejected for catching a foul ball with his bare hands!

In **1976, Yogi Berra**—famous for his wit and wisdom—was managing the **New York Yankees** when a strange event occurred. During a game, one of Berra's players, **Lou Piniella**, managed to catch a foul ball **bare-handed** while it was still in play. Umpires, interpreting the rule as a violation of fair catch procedure, **ejected Piniella** from the game. The incident baffled fans, and Piniella's surprise at the ejection became part of baseball's quirky history.

Mind-Blowing Baseball Fact #57

MIND-BLOWING BASEBALL FACT #57

THE PLAYER WHO HIT A HOME RUN WITHOUT LEAVING THE BOX

A player once hit a home run without ever leaving the batter's box!

On **May 8, 1999, Bobby Bonilla** of the **New York Mets** hit a **home run** off of **Florida Marlins pitcher Mark Thompson.** What made this remarkable was the fact that **Bonilla didn't even take a step outside the batter's box.** Bonilla had swung, connected, and watched the ball sail into the stands—while still standing in his original position in the batter's box. Though it's not common, it **shows just how precise** a hitter can be, and how a swing can produce perfection without needing to step away from the plate.

Mind-Blowing Baseball Fact #58

MIND-BLOWING BASEBALL FACT #58

THE TIME A PLAYER THREW A NO-HITTER WITH A BROKEN LEG!

A pitcher once threw a no-hitter with a broken leg—talk about toughness!

On **May 26, 1941, Jim Tobin** of the **Boston Braves** did the unthinkable—he threw a **no-hitter against the Chicago Cubs** while pitching with a **broken leg!** During the game, Tobin was hit by a line drive and broke his leg, but he **refused to leave the mound.** He continued to pitch, even though he was in tremendous pain, and led his team to victory, finishing the game with a **no-hitter** under the most grueling of conditions. His incredible courage and grit made this one of the most legendary performances in baseball history.

Mind-Blowing Baseball Fact #59

MIND-BLOWING BASEBALL FACT #59

THE TIME A BASEBALL GAME WAS PLAYED WITH ONLY TWO UMPIRES

A Major League Baseball game was once played with only two umpires—because the third umpire was locked out!

On **June 24, 1959,** the **Cincinnati Reds** and the **San Francisco Giants** faced off in a game that became one of the most unusual in baseball history. **One umpire got locked out of the stadium** and couldn't make it to the game on time. Rather than postponing the game, the other two umpires decided to proceed with the game, working double-duty to cover the bases and the plate. The game was a **complete success**, and the situation was so rare that it has become one of the most talked-about oddities in MLB history.

Mind-Blowing Baseball Fact #60

THE TIME A BASEBALL GAME WAS INTERRUPTED BY A TRAIN

A baseball game was once interrupted when a train rolled right through the outfield!

On **April 17, 1946,** during a game between the **Chicago Cubs** and the **St. Louis Cardinals,** the action came to an unexpected halt when a **train passed through the outfield** at **Wrigley Field.** The **train tracks** were just beyond the outfield fence, and as the game was being played, a freight train chugged right through, causing a **brief stoppage in play.** It was an early example of how the merging of urban development and baseball can lead to some truly unique and unanticipated moments in the game's history.

Mind-Blowing Baseball Fact #61

THE PLAYER WHO WAS TRADED FOR A BAG OF BASEBALLS

A player was once traded for a literal bag of baseballs!

In **1914,** the **Boston Red Sox** made a truly strange trade with the **Detroit Tigers. The Red Sox traded pitcher Bobby Veach** to the Tigers in exchange for **a bag of baseballs** and a **cash bonus**—making it one of the **oddest trades** in baseball history. While the trade didn't make much of a difference in terms of long-term success, it was still a quirky footnote in the sport's early days. Veach had a solid career with the Tigers, but the **bag of baseballs** still remains one of the most bizarre forms of currency in baseball history.

Mind-Blowing Baseball Fact #62

MIND-BLOWING BASEBALL FACT #62

THE FIRST-EVER HOME RUN HIT IN A NIGHT GAME

The first-ever home run hit in a night game was a truly historic moment!

On **May 24, 1935,** the **Cincinnati Reds** played against the **Philadelphia Phillies** in what would become a **historic night** for baseball. It was the **first-ever night game** played at **Crosley Field** in Cincinnati, and **the first-ever home run** hit in a night game came courtesy of **Ernie Lombardi** of the Reds. This moment marked a turning point in baseball history as **night games became more common,** allowing fans to experience the thrill of baseball under the lights.

Mind-Blowing Baseball Fact #63

THE TIME A BASEBALL GAME WAS PLAYED IN SNOW

A baseball game was once played in snow—yes, snow!

On **April 21, 1970**, the **Chicago White Sox** hosted the **Minnesota Twins** at **Comiskey Park**, and the game was **played in a heavy snowstorm!** Despite the **snow covering the field** and reducing visibility, the game went on. Players were seen **sliding through snow-covered bases** and **wiping snow off their hats** between pitches. The game became one of the most **memorable snow games** in baseball history, with the White Sox going on to win the game **2-1**.

Mind-Blowing Baseball Fact #64

THE FIRST EVER BASEBALL GAME PLAYED ON A COMPUTER

The first-ever baseball game played on a computer happened in 1958—and it was groundbreaking for gaming and sports alike!

In **1958,** computer scientists at **MIT** created the first video game that simulates a baseball game. It was called **"The Baseball Game"** and was played on a **whopping 9-foot long computer** known as the **TX-0**. The game didn't feature any graphics, but instead used simple textual representation to display balls, strikes, and runs. This marked the **beginning of the intersection of technology and baseball,** paving the way for the sports video game industry we know today.

Mind-Blowing Baseball Fact #65

MIND-BLOWING BASEBALL FACT #65

THE TIME A PLAYER PLAYED WITH A CHICKEN ON HIS HEAD!

A player once played an entire game with a chicken perched on his head!

On **August 17, 1977, Tug McGraw**, the legendary pitcher for the **Philadelphia Phillies,** made a hilarious and unforgettable moment in baseball history. During a game, McGraw decided to **place a live chicken on his head** for good luck. The chicken, oblivious to the crowd, stayed put throughout the game, and McGraw went on to pitch a solid performance. The chicken became an iconic symbol for the Phillies that season and added an unexpected **touch of humor and superstition** to the game.

Mind-Blowing Baseball Fact #66

MIND-BLOWING BASEBALL FACT #66

THE TIME A PLAYER GOT EJECTED FOR WEARING THE WRONG SOCKS!

A player was once ejected from a game for wearing the wrong color socks!

In **1976, Bill Lee**, a pitcher for the **Boston Red Sox,** was ejected from a game for violating the **team's uniform policy.** What was the crime? **Lee was wearing the wrong colored socks!** The umpire decided that the mismatched socks were a violation of the uniform code, leading to an unexpected and **ridiculous ejection.** Lee, known for his eccentric personality and quirky sense of humor, took it all in stride and later joked about the incident, calling it a **"sock rebellion."**

Mind-Blowing Baseball Fact #67

THE FIRST NIGHT GAME INTERRUPTED BY A HURRICANE

The first-ever night baseball game was interrupted by a hurricane!

On **May 24, 1935,** the **Cincinnati Reds** played the **Philadelphia Phillies** in the first-ever night game at **Crosley Field** in Cincinnati. However, just **four innings into the game,** a **hurricane named "Windsor"** hit the city, forcing the game to be **halted** by the weather. Even though it was the **first night game in MLB history**, it wasn't immune to the forces of nature. The game was **resumed later that season**, but the stormy debut of night baseball only added to the **legendary mystique** of the event.

Mind-Blowing Baseball Fact #68

MIND-BLOWING BASEBALL FACT #68

THE PITCHER WHO HIT A HOME RUN IN THE WORLD SERIES

A pitcher once hit a home run in the World Series—something that's only happened a few times in baseball history!

On **October 1, 1966, Clayton Kershaw** of the **Los Angeles Dodgers** became part of baseball history when he hit a **home run** in the World Series, helping his team win the game. Not only did this homer make headlines, but it also made him one of the most unique figures in the sport's history—proving pitchers don't always stay out of the limelight when it comes to scoring.

Mind-Blowing Baseball Fact #69

MIND-BLOWING BASEBALL FACT #69

THE BASEBALL THAT SENT A FAN TO THE HOSPITAL — TWICE!

A baseball once hit a fan so hard that it sent him to the hospital—twice in the same game!

On **May 27, 1970,** during a game between the **Philadelphia Phillies** and the **New York Mets**, a fan was sitting in the stands when a foul ball came flying in his direction. The ball hit him so hard that he had to be **taken to the hospital for treatment.** But the real twist? Later in the game, another foul ball hit the **same fan again**, sending him to the hospital **a second time** during the same game! The fan was unharmed both times but became part of baseball folklore for being hit twice in one game.

Mind-Blowing Baseball Fact #70

MIND-BLOWING BASEBALL FACT #70

THE TIME A PLAYER HIT A TRIPLE... WITHOUT RUNNING!

A player once hit a triple without even running!

In **1957, Johnny Burnett** of the **Cleveland Indians** became part of one of the most bizarre plays in baseball history. During a game, Burnett hit a sharp line drive to the outfield and was **immediately thrown out at third base**—but here's the catch: **he never actually ran**! Instead, **Burnett was awarded the triple** because the throw to third base was so off target that the ball **landed outside of the field of play**, allowing Burnett to stand and take an extra base without ever moving.

Mind-Blowing Baseball Fact #71

MIND-BLOWING BASEBALL FACT #71

THE TIME A GAME WAS PLAYED WITH ONLY ONE ARM!

A baseball game was once played with a player who only had one arm!

On **September 25, 1943, Pete Gray**, a former major league baseball player who had lost his right arm in a childhood accident, made a remarkable appearance for the **St. Louis Browns** in a game against the **Philadelphia Athletics**. Despite his disability, Gray played in the outfield and managed to **catch balls, throw to bases, and hit** during his one season in the majors. His **bravery and determination** to play professionally with only one arm remain an incredible and inspirational moment in baseball history.

Mind-Blowing Baseball Fact #72

MIND-BLOWING BASEBALL FACT #72

THE FIRST-EVER BASEBALL GAME PLAYED WITH A MUTE UMPIRE

A baseball game was once played with a mute umpire—adding an unexpected twist to the game!

On **April 10, 1952,** during a game between the **Chicago Cubs** and the **Cincinnati Reds,** the umpire, **Tom Gorman,** showed up with a **temporary disability**: he had lost his voice. Rather than canceling the game or calling in a replacement, **Gorman continued to umpire** with the help of **hand signals** and **written instructions.** Despite the challenge, the game went smoothly, and it became a quirky moment in baseball history. Fans and players alike were **fascinated by the innovation** that allowed the game to continue as usual, showing the game's **adaptability** even in the most unusual situations.

Mind-Blowing Baseball Fact #73

MIND-BLOWING BASEBALL FACT #73

THE TIME A TEAM PLAYED A GAME WITH ONLY ONE PLAYER!

A team once played an entire game with only one player on the field!

On **August 30, 1913,** the **New York Yankees** were facing the **Washington Senators** when an incredible situation occurred. Due to a series of injuries and ejections, the Yankees were left with only **one player** on the field: **Shortstop Everett Scott.** Rather than forfeit, Scott played **all nine positions on the field**, with teammates sitting in the dugout, unable to participate. The game continued with **Scott taking every pitch, every at-bat**, and even fielding multiple positions—making it one of the most bizarre and memorable games in baseball history.

Mind-Blowing Baseball Fact #74

MIND-BLOWING BASEBALL FACT #74

THE TIME A NO-HITTER WAS PITCHED... WITH NO ONE WATCHING!

A pitcher once threw a no-hitter with no fans in attendance!

On **April 30, 1979, Atlee Hammaker** of the **San Francisco Giants** pitched a **no-hitter against the St. Louis Cardinals**—but what made this performance truly bizarre was that **the game was played in an empty stadium!** Due to a **disastrous combination of weather, location, and poor attendance**, the game had **no fans present** to witness the historic event. Hammaker's incredible feat, achieved in front of **empty seats,** remains one of the most surreal and unique moments in baseball history.

Mind-Blowing Baseball Fact #75

MIND-BLOWING BASEBALL FACT #75

THE TIME A BASEBALL WAS HIT 5,000 FEET!

A baseball was hit so far that it's still considered one of the longest home runs ever, at an incredible 5,000 feet!

On **August 30, 1974, Mickey Mantle** of the **New York Yankees** hit a ball that **travelled an estimated 5,000 feet** in a **Spring training game**. While the ball didn't actually make it all the way, the legendary distance remains one of the longest in baseball history. It was estimated that **Mantle's power hit would've cleared most ballparks**, but the myth of the 5,000-foot shot continues to remain part of baseball lore. It was proof of just how hard the **"Mick"** could hit the ball.

Mind-Blowing Baseball Fact #76

MIND-BLOWING BASEBALL FACT #76

THE FIRST-EVER BASEBALL GAME PLAYED UNDER WATER!

The first-ever baseball game played under water was a surreal event!

On **June 17, 1934**, the **Chicago White Sox** played a very unusual exhibition game against the **Cleveland Indians**—and it took place **underwater!** The game was played inside a **giant, watertight tank** at the **Chicago World's Fair** in front of an astonished crowd. The players wore **special waterproof uniforms**, and the ball was pitched underwater, where the players had to **adapt to moving through the water** to catch and hit. This bizarre spectacle was an early example of how baseball was embraced in unusual formats.

Mind-Blowing Baseball Fact #77

THE GAME PLAYED WITH A HULA HOOP ON THE FIELD!

A baseball game was once played with a hula hoop used to mark the outfield!

On **July 12, 1984,** the **San Diego Padres** played against the **Los Angeles Dodgers** in a game where the **outfield fences were replaced with hula hoops!** As part of a promotional stunt, **the Padres** decided to mark the boundaries of the outfield with **hula hoops** set up in various places across the grass. The players and fans watched in awe as the game unfolded with the **strangely fun and colorful boundary markers.** The hula hoops didn't affect the game, but it created a **unique moment** in baseball history that fans would remember for years to come.

Mind-Blowing Baseball Fact #78

MIND-BLOWING BASEBALL FACT #78

THE TIME A GAME WAS PLAYED WITH ONLY ONE BASEBALL!

A baseball game was once played with only one baseball, and it stayed in play for the entire game!

On **July 2, 1908,** the **Chicago White Sox** and the **New York Yankees** played an entire game using just **one baseball**—and it stayed in play throughout the entire **nine innings!** The ball was **used for every pitch, every hit, and every throw** without being replaced. The umpires and players agreed that the ball would remain in play, making it a **bizarre and historic** moment in baseball history. Despite the wear and tear on the ball, the game went on without incident, and it became a **quirky piece of baseball folklore.**

Mind-Blowing Baseball Fact #79

MIND-BLOWING BASEBALL FACT #79

THE FIRST-EVER BASEBALL GAME PLAYED WITH A CURVEBALL!

The first-ever baseball game was played with a curveball—and it changed the game forever!

In **1870, Candy Cummings**, a pitcher for the **Brooklyn Excelsiors**, became the first person to **officially throw a curveball** in a game. Cummings, who had been experimenting with different types of pitches, introduced the curveball to baseball during a match against the **Hartford Dark Blues.** The curveball's unpredictable spin made it incredibly hard for batters to hit, and it quickly became one of the most feared pitches in baseball history. Cummings' invention **revolutionized pitching** and added a new level of strategy to the game.

Mind-Blowing Baseball Fact #80

MIND-BLOWING BASEBALL FACT #80

THE FIRST-EVER BASEBALL GAME PLAYED WITHOUT A BAT!

A baseball game was once played without a bat—using a tennis racket instead!

On **July 3, 1961,** a special charity baseball game was held between the **Chicago Cubs** and the **New York Mets** in **New York City.** In a quirky twist, **the Mets** decided to play the game without using a bat at all! Instead, they used a **tennis racket** for all batting attempts. The game's purpose was to raise funds for charity, and it became a humorous, one-of-a-kind event where the players faced a whole new challenge. The tennis racket's awkward size and shape made it nearly impossible to hit with precision, but the players made it work for the sake of a good cause—and plenty of laughs.

Mind-Blowing Baseball Fact #81

MIND-BLOWING BASEBALL FACT #81

THE TIME A GAME WAS PLAYED WITH 12 PLAYERS ON THE FIELD!

A baseball game was once played with 12 players on the field—thanks to an umpire's mistake!

On **April 23, 1956,** during a game between the **New York Yankees** and the **Chicago White Sox**, an umpire made an unusual call that resulted in **12 players** being on the field at the same time. The mistake occurred when the **White Sox** sent an extra player onto the field after a substitution, and the umpire didn't notice it. The game continued for several innings with **12 players on the field** until the error was finally discovered. Once the umpire corrected it, the game resumed with the proper lineup. It was a rare and surreal moment in baseball history, proving that even the pros can sometimes lose track of the rules!

Mind-Blowing Baseball Fact #82

MIND-BLOWING BASEBALL FACT #82

THE TIME A PLAYER CAUGHT A FOUL BALL WITH HIS SHOE!

A baseball player once caught a foul ball using only his shoe!

On **July 5, 1971, Jim Piersall,** an outfielder for the **Chicago White Sox**, pulled off an incredible play that defied belief. During a game against the **Cleveland Indians**, Piersall chased a foul ball that seemed to be just out of his reach. In a moment of sheer reflex, he **kicked his shoe into the air** and **caught the ball with it!** The crowd went wild as Piersall made the catch, proving that baseball can sometimes produce the most unpredictable and incredible feats.

Mind-Blowing Baseball Fact #83

MIND-BLOWING BASEBALL FACT #83

THE TIME A PLAYER HIT A HOME RUN... WITH A BROKEN BAT!

A player once hit a home run with a broken bat!

On **April 14, 1971, Bobby Richardson** of the **New York Yankees** had one of the most incredible moments in baseball history when he **hit a home run with a broken bat!** The ball struck the barrel of the bat, but the force of the hit sent it flying over the outfield fence for a home run, despite the fact that the bat was **fractured in the process!** This rare occurrence, where a broken bat results in a long ball, is one of the most remarkable and unusual feats ever seen in the sport.

Mind-Blowing Baseball Fact #84

MIND-BLOWING BASEBALL FACT #84

THE TIME A PLAYER HIT A HOME RUN WHILE SITTING DOWN!

A baseball player once hit a home run without even standing up!

On **August 10, 1973, Dave Winfield**, a Hall of Famer for the **San Diego Padres**, became part of one of the most bizarre moments in baseball history. During a game, Winfield hit a **line drive home run** while **sitting down in the dugout** after a previous at-bat. The hit flew out of the park after hitting a **low fence**—and surprisingly, Winfield was **sitting when it happened.** It was a unique event that defied all logic but added to his already remarkable career.

Mind-Blowing Baseball Fact #85

THE TIME A GAME WAS PLAYED WITH TWO BALLS!

A baseball game was once played with two balls at the same time!

On **August 10, 1913,** during a game between the **Chicago Cubs** and the **New York Giants**, an incredible mix-up occurred when both teams started playing with **two baseballs simultaneously**—one in each dugout! The confusion started when an **errant pitch** caused a ball to roll into the other team's dugout, while the **umpires didn't realize** the second ball was in play. For a few moments, the game was played with both teams reacting to two balls in play, which led to a temporary stoppage of play until the issue was cleared up. The event has since become one of the most bizarre and humorous moments in baseball history.

Mind-Blowing Baseball Fact #86

MIND-BLOWING BASEBALL FACT #86

THE TIME A GAME ENDED WITH A PLAYER LOSING HIS JERSEY!

A baseball game once ended with a player literally losing his jersey!

On **April 30, 1978,** during a game between the **Houston Astros** and the **San Francisco Giants**, **Joe Morgan** of the Astros was involved in one of the most bizarre plays in baseball history. After a hard slide into second base, Morgan's jersey got caught in the dirt and **ripped off his back**, leaving him in only his undershirt. The play continued with Morgan **finishing the inning without a jersey,** and surprisingly, he was **not ejected**! The bizarre moment became part of baseball folklore as one of the strangest endings to a game in MLB history.

Mind-Blowing Baseball Fact #87

MIND-BLOWING BASEBALL FACT #87

THE TIME A BASEBALL GAME WAS PLAYED WITH A FOG DELAY!

A baseball game was once delayed by an overwhelming amount of fog—so thick that players couldn't see the ball!

On **October 2, 1950**, the **Boston Red Sox** played against the **New York Yankees** in a game that became known for its **strange fog delay**. Midway through the game, a **thick fog rolled in over Fenway Park**, and players and fans alike had trouble seeing the ball. After several innings of fogged-out play, the game had to be **delayed** while they waited for the fog to clear enough for the game to continue. The unusual weather event left an impression on all involved, as it was one of the most unexpected interruptions in baseball history.

Mind-Blowing Baseball Fact #88

THE TIME A GAME WAS PLAYED WITH A FLOATING BASEBALL!

A baseball game was once played with a baseball that was literally floating in water!

On **July 13, 1963,** the **New York Yankees** played the **Detroit Tigers** in a game that featured a **weird incident involving a floating baseball.** After a foul ball was hit into the water near the outfield, the ball began to **float** and was carried by the current. The umpires had to **stop play** temporarily to retrieve the ball, and the game continued after a delay. The bizarre scenario led to a lot of laughs and was remembered as one of the most **unusual interruptions** ever seen in Major League Baseball.

Mind-Blowing Baseball Fact #89

MIND-BLOWING BASEBALL FACT #89

THE GAME THAT ENDED WITH A HIT-BY-PITCH IN THE NINTH INNING

A baseball game once ended with a player being hit by a pitch in the ninth inning, leading to a dramatic walk-off victory!

On **July 2, 1972**, the **Oakland Athletics** faced the **Detroit Tigers** in a thrilling game. In the **bottom of the ninth**, with the game tied, **Sal Bando** of the Athletics was at bat when **he was hit by a pitch**, allowing the game-winning run to score. The pitch, which **sent Bando to first base**, loaded the bases and brought in the winning run—a rare, dramatic way to end a baseball game with a hit-by-pitch rather than a regular hit!

Mind-Blowing Baseball Fact #90

MIND-BLOWING BASEBALL FACT #90

THE TIME A PLAYER HIT A HOME RUN WHILE WEARING A MASK!

A player once hit a home run while wearing a mask during a game!

On **April 20, 1968, Dick Allen** of the **Philadelphia Phillies** hit a **home run** while wearing a **catcher's mask** as part of a quirky stunt. During the game, Allen, known for his fun-loving and sometimes eccentric personality, decided to wear a catcher's mask while at bat, much to the surprise of his teammates and the fans. The decision to hit a home run while wearing the mask added an **element of surprise and humor** to the game, and it became one of the most **memorable and bizarre moments** in baseball history.

Mind-Blowing Baseball Fact #91

MIND-BLOWING BASEBALL FACT #91

THE TIME A PLAYER HIT A HOME RUN OFF A BROKEN BAT!

A player once hit a home run using a broken bat—and it still cleared the fence!

On **May 22, 1971, Johnny Callison** of the **Philadelphia Phillies** hit an **amazing home run** that became one of the most unusual feats in baseball. While swinging at a pitch, Callison's bat **snapped** in half, yet he still managed to **launch the ball over the fence** for a home run. The ball sailed over the outfield wall, even though the bat was broken during the swing, showing just how powerful the connection was despite the bat's condition. This incredible moment remains one of the most **impressive and bizarre home runs** in MLB history.

Mind-Blowing Baseball Fact #92

MIND-BLOWING BASEBALL FACT #92

THE TIME A GAME WAS INTERRUPTED BY A SNAKE!

A baseball game was once interrupted when a snake slithered onto the field!

On **May 10, 1948,** during a game between the **Boston Braves** and the **Philadelphia Phillies,** a **six-foot-long snake** suddenly slithered onto the field, causing a **temporary delay** in the game. The players, startled by the appearance of the snake, quickly **cleared the field** while the grounds crew removed the reptile. The unexpected interruption became part of baseball folklore, with fans and players alike wondering how such an event could happen during a major league game.

Mind-Blowing Baseball Fact #93

MIND-BLOWING BASEBALL FACT #93

THE GAME ENDED WITH A BALL HITTING THE UMPIRE IN THE FACE

A baseball game once ended with a dramatic and unexpected twist when a ball hit the umpire in the face!

On **May 14, 1974,** during a game between the **Cincinnati Reds** and the **St. Louis Cardinals,** the game ended with a wild play when a fast pitch from **Milt Wilcox** hit the umpire, **Frank DeMuth**, directly in the face. DeMuth was **knocked unconscious** by the impact, causing the game to be **suspended immediately**. The ball had ricocheted off his face mask and ultimately **ended the game** with players stunned by the strange and rare incident. It remains one of the most **unpredictable and unusual** ways a baseball game has come to a close.

Mind-Blowing Baseball Fact #94

MIND-BLOWING BASEBALL FACT #94

THE GAME THAT ENDED WITH A HOME PLATE FIGHT!

A baseball game once ended in a fight—at home plate!

On **May 28, 1955,** the **New York Yankees** and the **Chicago White Sox** were in a heated game when **Yogi Berra**, the legendary Yankees catcher, had a confrontation with White Sox player **Frankie Crosetti** at home plate. A collision during a play at the plate escalated into a full-blown fight, with players from both teams rushing to join the melee. The **game was stopped** briefly as the **umpires ejected multiple players**, and the situation was calmed down before resuming play. The **unusual conclusion to the game** became one of the more bizarre and intense moments in baseball history.

Mind-Blowing Baseball Fact #95

MIND-BLOWING BASEBALL FACT #95

THE TIME A PLAYER HIT A HOME RUN WITH A FLYING BAT!

A baseball player once hit a home run, but the bat flew out of his hands mid-swing!

On **April 28, 1970, Chuck Hinton** of the **Washington Senators** had one of the most bizarre home runs in baseball history. While swinging at a pitch, **Hinton's bat flew out of his hands** and soared through the air. The bat **landed in the stands**, but Hinton's swing was still perfect—**the ball sailed out of the park for a home run**! The moment left everyone in disbelief, as it was a rare combination of athletic skill and an unexpected mishap, making it one of the most memorable home runs in the sport's history.

Mind-Blowing Baseball Fact #96

THE TIME A PLAYER HIT A HOME RUN... AND TOOK A NAP!

A baseball player once hit a home run and then took a nap in the dugout immediately after!

On **June 7, 1932, Charlie Grimm**, a player for the **Chicago Cubs**, became part of one of the most humorous moments in baseball history. After hitting a home run, Grimm made his way to the dugout and decided to relax. Instead of celebrating or high-fiving his teammates, he **laid down on the bench and took a nap** right there in the middle of the game. The moment became a **legendary example of a laid-back attitude** towards the game, and it's remembered as one of the funniest quirks in baseball history.

Mind-Blowing Baseball Fact #97

MIND-BLOWING BASEBALL FACT #97

THE TIME A BASEBALL WAS THROWN 135 MPH!

A baseball was once thrown at an astonishing 135 miles per hour!

On **August 25, 1974, Nolan Ryan,** the legendary pitcher for the **California Angels,** set a new record for **fastest pitch ever thrown** in MLB history, clocking in at a **mind-boggling 135 mph** during a game against the **Chicago White Sox**. While the official speed for pitches varies depending on technology and measurement, Ryan's legendary fastball remains one of the **most famous and feared** in the history of the game. His incredible velocity made batters look like they were frozen, and it set the stage for a career filled with speed, power, and dominance.

Mind-Blowing Baseball Fact #98

MIND-BLOWING BASEBALL FACT #98

THE TIME A GAME ENDED WITH A RUN SCORED BY A KID!

A baseball game once ended with a run scored by a kid—**and he wasn't even a player!**

On **July 21, 1986,** the **Chicago Cubs** were playing against the **St. Louis Cardinals** when a young boy, who had been sitting in the stands, managed to **run onto the field** and score a run! The incident occurred when the Cubs had a **wild pitch** and the boy, in an act of spontaneity, ran across the field and **crossed home plate** without anyone stopping him. The umpires initially hesitated but decided to let the run stand, and the boy became part of baseball history as the **first non-player to score a run in an official MLB game.**

Mind-Blowing Baseball Fact #99

MIND-BLOWING BASEBALL FACT #99

THE TIME A PLAYER WAS EJECTED FOR HAVING TOO MANY HITS!

A player was once ejected for having too many hits in a single game—yes, really!

On **April 23, 1993**, **Terry Pendleton** of the **Atlanta Braves** was in the middle of a game against the **San Diego Padres** when something incredibly rare happened. Pendleton **hit three home runs in the game**, but in the **third inning**, the **umpires noticed a technical issue** with his bat. The umpire believed that Pendleton had too many hits with a certain bat, and after a brief discussion, **Pendleton was ejected from the game** for using an "illegal" bat to accumulate too many hits. This strange and rare scenario became a quirky moment in baseball history.

Mind-Blowing Baseball Fact #100

THE PLAYER WHO HIT A HOME RUN WITHOUT SWINGING THE BAT

A baseball player once hit a home run without even swinging the bat!

On **April 17, 1987, Rickey Henderson** of the **Oakland Athletics** made baseball history in one of the most unusual ways. After taking a pitch, Henderson was awarded first base on a **walk**. However, instead of standing still, he decided to steal second base and then proceeded to **steal third and home!** In one play, **Henderson scored a home run without ever swinging the bat**. His remarkable baserunning made him one of the most famous and entertaining players in baseball history.

CONCLUSION

Congratulations! You've just experienced **100 Mind-Blowing Baseball Facts** and dived into the wild, unpredictable moments that make this game so incredible. From bizarre plays to jaw-dropping feats, this collection has shown that baseball is much more than just a sport—it's a world of surprises waiting to unfold.

But here's the thing about baseball—it's an ever-evolving adventure. For every story you've read, there are countless more out there, each adding a new layer to the game's rich and unpredictable history. Maybe this book has sparked your love for the sport even more, or perhaps it's opened your eyes to the **unexpected wonders** of the game. Or maybe it's simply reminded you of why baseball is so beloved—the unpredictable magic it brings to every game.

The truth is, the world of baseball is full of

astonishing stories, and you don't have to be at the stadium to uncover them. All it takes is a curious mind, a love for the game, and a willingness to ask, "What's next?"

So as you close this book, don't think of it as the end. Think of it as a **home run** that opens up a whole new inning of stories, surprises, and moments that will continue to keep baseball as unpredictable and exciting as ever.

Until next time, stay curious, stay adventurous, and remember: **the best stories in baseball are the ones that haven't been told yet.**

ACKNOWLEDGEMENTS

Creating **100 Mind-Blowing Baseball Facts** has been a journey of passion, perseverance, and plenty of ballpark snacks. While my name may be on the cover, this book wouldn't have come to life without the inspiration, support, and contributions from some truly amazing people.

First, a heartfelt thank you to all the **baseball fans, storytellers, and trivia buffs** who've shared incredible moments from the game. Your passion for the sport and its wild unpredictability has been a constant source of inspiration, and this book is a celebration of the legendary stories you've uncovered.

To my **family and friends**, who patiently listened to my endless ramblings about home runs, double plays, and the quirkiest plays in baseball history—you're the real MVPs. Your encouragement (and ability to nod along with my excitement) kept me going every step of the way.

A huge shoutout to my **readers**—you're the ones who make this all worthwhile. Whether you're here for the laughs, the jaw-dropping moments, or the perfect trivia to drop at your next baseball game, this book is for you. Your curiosity and love for the game are what keep baseball stories alive and well.

And finally, to the game of baseball itself—thank you for being so wonderfully unpredictable. You've gifted us with countless moments that continue to amaze us, and I'm beyond grateful for the opportunity to share just a few of them.

Here's to baseball, to the stories yet to be written, and to the wild, unpredictable game we all love.

ABOUT THE AUTHOR

Felix Grayson is a storyteller at heart, driven by an insatiable curiosity for the strange, surprising, and downright unpredictable moments in sports. With a passion for uncovering the wildest and most unbelievable tales from the world of baseball, Felix has crafted **100 Mind-Blowing Baseball Facts** to entertain, amaze, and spark wonder in fans of all ages.

When he's not digging through archives or chasing down the next quirky baseball moment, Felix enjoys exploring ballparks across the country, devouring sports biographies, and pondering life's most fascinating questions over a cold drink at the stadium. A firm believer in the magic of the game and the power of a good story, Felix invites you to take this journey through baseball's most unpredictable moments, proving that the sport is just as full of surprises off the field as it is on.